KOLMER FAMILY HISTORY

GERMANY TO AMERICA

By

Katherine Fletcher

KOLMER FAMILY NAME ORIGIN

The Kolmer family name comes from various parts of Germany.   There are also Kolmer names found in Scotland and Ireland.   This line comes from Germany. Kolmer's were also found in the Netherlands, Canada and

INTRODUCTION

This Kolmer lines comes from Germany to America in the mid 1800s.   They settled in Baltimore Maryland and other branches went on to Salem, Virginia, Texas and other locations in the United States.

Baltimore was a major entry port for immigrants from Germany.   In the 1700s they began to settle along the Chesapeake Bay which is the same area that would later become Baltimore in 1729.   These 18th century immigrants started the German Society of Maryland in 1793.   After the War of 1812 German immigrants came in groups from Hesse, Bavaria, Bohemia and Palatinate. Many fled to avoid being forced into the Royal German Military.   They also created a German language newspaper called Baltimore Wrecker.   Another wave of immigration to Baltimore came around 1848 due the Revolutions happening in Germany.

Many of these German immigrants were Jewish and created Yiddish theatres and synagogues.   The Jewish people living in Baltimore were from Bavarian and Hessian descent.

GENERATION ONE

Dr. George August Leonard (1881-1954)   and Emma Cameron Cook (1898-1982)

He was also married to Annie Arnold Palmer   (1876-1930)

Dr. George was born May 15, 1881 in Lonaconing, Allegany, Maryland and died November 21, 1954 in Salem, Culpepper, Virginia.

Emma Cook was born April 23, 1898 in Roanoke, VA and died November 4, 1982 in Salem, VA

Emma's parents are John Wilson Cook and Julie King Cook. John was from Pennsylvania. Emma's father John was married four times and she had many half siblings. Emma's grandparents are Henry Cook and Mary A. Hollowbush from Pennsylvania. The family is originally from England.

Dr. George Kolmer, Active In Salem Affairs, Dies at 70

Dr. George A. L. Kolmer, 70, vice president of Farmers National Bank, Salem, and a trustee of Roanoke College, died yesterday at his home at 228 Richfield Ave., Salem.

For a number of years, Dr. Kolmer served as health officer for the Town of Salem and as Roanoke County medical examiner. He had practiced in Salem for 40 years.

* * *

ACTIVE in both civic and medical affairs, he was appointed to the board of directors of Farmers National Bank in 1915. In 1936 he was elected vice president.

He was a lieutenant colonel in the Army Medical Corps in World War II, and also served as a medical officer in World War I. He was a past commander of Salem Post 19 of the American Legion.

Dr. Kolmer was a charter member of Salem Kiwanis Club and a member of College Lutheran Church.

* * *

IN ADDITION to his medical degree he held an LL.B. degree from the University of Maryland.

He is survived by his widow, Mrs. Emma Cook Kolmer; two sons, George Jr., in the Army at Ft. Jackson, S.C., and J. W. Kolmer, a student at Hampden-Sydney College; a daughter, Mary Cook Kolmer, a student at Salem College, Winston-Salem, N.C.; three brothers, Dr. John A. Kolmer, Philadelphia, Pa.; Leonard E. Kolmer and Harold S. Kolmer, both of Baltimore and a sister, Mrs. George Karn of Baltimore.

Funeral will be at 10:30 a.m.

Dr. G. A. L. Kolmer
(picture taken about 1944)

tomorrow at College Lutheran Church conducted by the Rev. M. L. Minnick, assisted by the Rev. Frederick Griffith. Burial will be in Sherwood.

Pallbearers will be Dr. Harry I. Johnson, Dr. John A. Gardner, C. E. Webber, E. H. Loud, Norman R. Moore, Keith K. Hunt, Dr. Thad McCulloch and Dr. Hugh Lee.

The body will be at the John M. Oakey Funeral Home until one hour before service.

The family has requested flowers be omitted.

Advertise

Children:

Col. Dr. John Wilson Kolmer 1933-2003 buried at Arlington National cemetery in VA.   married Mary Ann Wright.

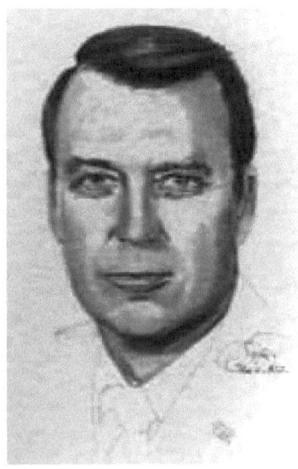

George Jr.   in the army at ft. Jackson SC

Mary Cook Kolmer

GENERATION TWO

Leonard Kolmer (1853 Germany)   and Selma Louise
Reichart (1860)

Seventy-Five Years of Marriage Their Total

MRS. JOSEPH MILLER — MR. AND MRS. LEONARD KOLMER — JOSEPH MILLER

Leonard Kolmer NY Passenger   List information:

Name: Leonard Kolmer
[Leonard Kolmer]
Arrival Date: 3 Sep 1890
Birth Date: abt 1848
Age: 42
Gender: Male
Ethnicity/ Nationality: German
Place of Origin: Germany
Port of Departure: Antwerp, Belgium
Destination: New York
Port of Arrival: New York, New York
Ship Name: Friesland

Selma Louise Reichart

SELMA LOUISE was born in Maryland 1860.   Her parents were Carl August Frederick Reichelt and Youstina Rosenia Frische.   Carl was from Dagnstadt, Germany and died in Kaiser, Maryland .   This lines goes back to Annaberg, Chemnitz, Sachsen, Germany.

Their Children:

Dr. George August Leonard Kolmer   1881-1954 married Selma Louise Reichart

Rosina Justine   1884-1951   married Joseph Miller / Baltimore, Maryland

Dr. John Albert Kolmer, Philadelphia, PA (1886-1962) married Cecilia Herron.   He was professor of medicine at Temple University and won a 1929 Mendel Medal. He developed a vaccine for infantile paralysis.   Also referred to as a blood specialist.

Leonard Eckert Kolmer - Baltimore   (1889-1963) married Marie Lasseter and Idella Skillman Kizer (married 1954). He was the business manager of the Frederick Post, Frederick, Maryland.   He was a Lieutenant in the WW   / also General Manager of the Auto Club of Maryland.   I found his obituary which said he was also a reporter for the SUN until WWI.   After the war he started a newspaper brokerage firm in Richmond.   He sold newspaper machinery and negotiated mergers.   He returned to Baltimore in 1933.   He died at a Christmas Party. He was buried at St. Paul's Lutheran Cemetery in

Violetville.

Marie (Mamie) Kolmer   1892-1973 married George C. Karn

Harold Smith Kolmer   - Baltimore   1895-1965 married Loretta Clary/ served in WWII/ secretary of Maryland State Game and Inland Fish Commission.

William

GENERATION THREE

Johann Georg Kolmer (1816-before 1881) and Margaretha Anna Eckert (1822-1883)

Birth 24 OCT 1816 in Zotzenbach, Germany .   He was a farmer.   He died in Germany.

Margaretha Eckert was born 15 SEP 1822 in Mengelbach, Germany / died in Maryland.   She immigrated to America with her son John in 1881. The ship was named the Baltimore. They departed from Bremen, Germany. She died in 1883.

Oak Hill—Grandmother Kolmer's Grave

Their children:

Adam Kolmer   - 1883   born in Germany, died in Maryland

Elizabeth

John   1865-1917 Preuse, Germany to Indianapolis, Indiana / also a Doctor.   He worked many jobs when he got to America including farming, coal mining, clerk in a general store at Eckhart Mines.   He went to Indiana in 1886. He worked in the druggist sundries business and continued studying medicine.   He graduated in 1894 from historic Old Jefferson Medical College and later recieved Doctorate of Medicine.   He interned at Jefferson Hospital in Philadelphia and St. Joseph's Hospital in Reading, PA.   In 1896 he returned to Indianapolis.   In 1899 he made a trip to Germany and did post graduate work in hospitals and medical schools in Berlin, Heidelberg, Vienna and Munich.   He came back to the U.S. in 1899 to live in Indianapolis with a private practice. He was also a Knights Templar and reached the 32nd level of the Ancient Scottish Rite. He was also part of the ancient Arabic Order of the Nobles of the Mystic Shrine, as well as a member of the Knights of Pythias.   An article I found said he was one of the first surgeons to operate on children for criminal intent.   What does this mean? He married May Aufderheide of Indianapolis.

JOHN KOLMER M D

DOCTOR JOHN KOLMER
Surgeon

Club Men of Indianapolis in Caricature, 1913

Katherine married Nickolas Fuhr and remained in Germany

Egnidius   1846-   / married Anna Katharina Volz / he was

a cabinetmaker and also stayed in Germany

Leonard Eckhart   1853 –1932   married Emma Cameron Cook/ born in Berlin Germany, died in Baltimore, Maryland

GENERATION FOUR

Johann Peter Kolmer   1780-1837 and Eva Maria Getrosch (1784)

Birth 9 AUG 1780 in Waldmichelbach, Germany

Their children:

Johann Georg   1816 –before 1881 married Margaretha Eckert

Anna Catherine

GENERATION FIVE

Georg Leonhard Collmer 1732-1746   and Anna Katharina

Birth 18 AUG 1732 in Waldmichelbach, Germany

Death   1746 in Waldmichelbach, Germany

Their children:

Anna Katharine Kollmar   1767-1807 married Johannes Mund

GENERATION SIX

Leonard Colmer   1702-1746 and Marie Katharine

> Affolterbach Bergstrasse, Hessen,, Germany

Their children:

Johanne George Leonard Kollmer

GENERATION SEVEN

Christoffel Kolmer   1667-1729 and Margaretha

> Birth 8 DEC 1667 in Affolterbach, Germany

Their children:

Leonhard Collmar   1702-1746

GENERATION EIGHT

Anthoni Kolmer 1637-1693 and Magdalena Collmar

> Birth 24 Sep 1637 in Thierachem, Bern, Germany

Death about 1693 in Wahlen, Bergstrasse, Hessen, Germany

Looks like Anthoni was listed in the Military and marine records of Germany

Their children:

Christoffel Kolmer   1667-1729

GENERATION NINE

Hans Kolmer 1607-   and Katharina Wenger

Their children:

Anthoni Kolmer – 1637-1693

Maria Collmar   - 1693

Simon   1630- / also listed in Germany list of Military and Marine

Anni   1631-

Elfi   1635-

German Empire from 1871-1919

THE KOLMERS AND THE KNIGHTS TEMPLAR, FREE MASONS AND ORDER OF THE ILLUMANATI

I was struck by one of the descendants above whose obituary mentioned his heavy involvement and high status in the order of the Knights Templar.   He also was on a 32 level of the Scottish Rite which indicates magic and other strange rituals.   These organizations were filled with unusual religious beliefs and even spells and magic. They are often passed on from fathers to sons through the generations. There is so much controversy about the Illuminati in terms of if they were atheists, Satanists or Christians.

The order of the Illuminati was founded by a man named Adam Weishaupt.   His goal was to replace Christianity with a religion of reason.   Adam was born Jewish but his family converted to Catholism.   He was for a brief time a priest and later an atheist.   He studied the writings of Voltaire which helped form his ideas about the destruction of the church.   He also travelled to France and met Robespierre, the leader of the French Revolution. While in France, he met a few people in the French Royal court who introduced him to Satanism. He also studied the teachings of astrology, medicine and magic.   Adam later became a Professor of Civil Law and Canon Law at the University of Ingolstadt.   The headquarters of the Illuminati was in Munich, Germany.   This group were hardly moral and righteous.   They used bribery and blackmail and other not so moral deeds.

He met a man named Franz Kolmer in 1770, a Danish merchant from Jutland.   Jutland is an area on the border of Denmark and West Germany.   The West Germany connection makes me wonder if he is related to this line of Kolmers and their long connection to Knights Templar and similar organizations.

  This Franz Kolmer had travelled around Europe and took many trips to Egypt. He also lived in Alexandria, Egypt for several years.   He studied the secret cults of Pythagoreans and the Eleusinian mysteries. Kolmer indoctrinated Adam into Egyptian occult practices. Pythagoras lived in the 6th century B.C. and was a philosopher who believed that men and women should combine their belongings.   This later became the premise for Communism. The Illuminati was an occult German group in the 15th century that claimed to possess the light of Satan.   It was also influenced by a writer named Emanuel Swedenborg which was started in Avignon in 1760.

There were other Illumist type groups throughout history. Adam Weisgarber certainly wasn't the first one with these ideas.   There was a group founded by a man named Jaochim of Floris known as the Illuminated Ones in the 11th century.   There was another group called the Rosheniah or Illuminated Ones in Afghanistan in the 16th century.   In Spain in the 16th century there was a movement call the Alumbrados.   They believed that when a person reached a certain level of perfection they would have a direct vision of God and communications with God.   History says that most of these groups were originally Franciscans and Jesuits.